Countdown to 2000

A Kid's Guide to the New Millennium

Bonnie Bader and Tracey West

Illustrated by Brad Teare

GIBBS·SMITH PUBLISHER

SALT LAKE CITY

First edition

99 98 97 96 5 4 3 2 1

This is a Peregrine Smith Book, published by
Gibbs Smith, Publisher
P.O. Box 667
Layton, Utah 84041

Design by Leesha Gibby Jones

Printed and Bound in Korea

Library of Congress Cataloging-in-Publication Data

Bader, Bonnie, 1961-
    Countdown to 2000: a kid's guide to the new millennium/
Bonnie Bader and Tracey West: illustrated by Brad Teare. —1st ed.
        p.   cm.
    ISBN 0-87905-729-7
    1. Two thousand, A.D.—Study and teaching—Activity programs.
I. West, Tracey, 1965-   . II. Teare, Brad, 1956-   . III. Title.
CB161.B34 1996
909.83—dc20   95-36304
                                         CIP
                                         AC

CONTENTS

Fun Stuff To Do!

To David and Lauren,
my guides to the new millennium.
B. B.

To my mom, Carole Klaver,
and my dad, Thomas Lubben,
for teaching me to love to read.
T. W.

To Ashley
B. T.

WHAT'S THE BIG DEAL?

If you're a human being (which you probably are) and you live on planet Earth (which you probably do), chances are you've been hearing about the year 2000 and "the new millennium." And like most humans on planet Earth, you're probably wondering what all the fuss is about.

The last time there was a new millennium, people got a little excited about it. Well, that's not exactly true—they got <u>really</u> excited about it. And this millennium probably won't be any different.

By now you're probably asking yourself intelligent questions such as, "2000 <u>what</u>?" and, "What is a millennium, anyway?" That's where this book comes in. It will answer all your questions about the big dates, plus give you tons of stuff to do while you're waiting for the new age to dawn. You'll want to keep it handy to record the events, thoughts, people, and predictions in the next few years of your life.

So what are you waiting for? It'll be the year 2000 before you know it!

WHAT IS A MILLENNIUM, ANYWAY?

A **millennium** is a period of one thousand years. The word comes from the Latin words *mille* (which means "a thousand") and *annus* (which means "year"): one thousand years.

So when people talk about "the new millennium," they mean that in the year 2001, the world will enter a new period of one thousand years. The last period (the one we're in now) began in the year 1001 and will end in 2000. Got it so far?

Hi! I'm Ralph, and I'm a MILLIPEDE.
I was named that because it looks
like I have a thousand legs.
(I really have about two hundred,
but who's counting?)

SO IT'S TWO THOUSAND YEARS SINCE <u>WHEN</u>?

This question is a little bit trickier to answer. First, you've got to understand something about dates and calendars.

You probably use calendars to remind you when your best friend's birthday is or to let you know when the first (or last) day of school will be. Well, about five thousand years ago, people decided they needed calendars so they would know when to plant their crops and when to get ready for winter.

WHAT DOES THIS HAVE TO DO WITH THE YEAR 2000?

We're almost there. About two thousand years after people first started keeping calendars, the Romans got the idea to give each passing year a number. Numbering years would make it easier to keep a record of events, such as when people were born and when battles were lost or won.

The Romans said the year one should be the year when the Roman Empire was founded. Most people liked that idea (since most of them were Romans), and so they named the years one after the other for about twelve hundred years.

That's when things changed. During those twelve hundred years, the Christian religion had grown to include many people and parts of the world. A Christian monk named Dionysius Exiguus decided the year one should begin on the birthday of Jesus Christ, who Christians worship as the son of God. Most people accepted his idea, and it's been that way ever since.

Anything that happened before the new year one is labeled **B.C.**, which stands for *before Christ*. Anything that happens after the year one is labeled **A.D.**, which stands for *anno domini*, a Latin phrase meaning "the year of our Lord."

When Dionysius named the new year 1, it was about the year 1200 in the Roman calendar. Dionysius said that Christ was born about 527 years before that year, so that meant the year Dionysius was living in was now called 527 A.D.

So that brings us to the present, almost to the year 2000 A.D.—two thousand years after the birth of Christ. A new millennium officially begins in the year 2001. But the year 2000, which closes out our current millennium, promises to be a celebratory year. (It won't be easy to remember to write *20__* when you date your school papers!) So this book celebrates both years—2000 and 2001.

7

WAIT JUST ONE SECOND...

Though most calendars you see will tell you we're close to the year 2000, those calendars don't tell you the whole story. There are many people in the world who don't follow a Christian religion, so their calendars aren't based on Christ's birthday. When we're celebrating the year 2000, it will be the year 1420 in the Moslem calendar. And in the Jewish calendar, it will be the year 5760!

Even the Christian calendar isn't perfect. Some experts think that old Dionysius Exiguus may have gotten Christ's birthday wrong. They think the birth actually happened about four years earlier. That means the *real* year 2000 would be in the year we call 1996!

Think you've got it? Great! Now it's time to find out just what this new millennium holds in store for all of us. Fast forward to the future...

MAKE A TIME CAPSULE

The new millennium might be only a few years away, but a lot can happen to you in a few years! Making a time capsule will help you keep a record of your life before the new millennium. Here's how to do it:

1. Collect a bunch of stuff that describes what your life is like now. Your class picture, a ticket stub from a sporting event or arts performance, and an empty box of your favorite cereal are all good things to put in a time capsule. Add pictures you've drawn of things you like (and don't like), too.

2. Put all the stuff into a cardboa.d box. Seal the box tightly with tape. Make sure you label the box with the date and the year you made it. Decorate it for fun.

3. Put the box in a safe place, such as a closet or an attic. On New Year's Day in the year 2001, open your time capsule! Is your life still the same as it was when you made the capsule?

I'm making a tape of all my favorite songs for my time capsule!

TIME CAPSULE LOG

Why not make a time capsule every year between now and the year 2001? Keep a record of the contents and locations of your capsules here so you won't forget.

TIME CAPSULE #1: _____

_____

Date finished: _____

Where to find it: _____

TIME CAPSULE #2: _____

_____

Date finished: _____

Where to find it: _____

TIME CAPSULE #3: _____

_____

Date finished: _____

Where to find it: _____

TIME CAPSULE #4: _____

_____

Date finished: _____

Where to find it: _____

TIME CAPSULE #5: _____

_____

Date finished: _____

Where to find it: _____

VISIONS OF THE FUTURE

So what will the new millennium be like? Humans have always tried to get a glimpse at what the future holds.

Take prophets, for example. Prophets are people who make predictions about what the future will be like. Prophets get their information from interesting sources, such as spirits or dreams. Some even say they get their knowledge from God.

Scientists also like to make predictions. They get their information from more down-to-earth sources, including studies, observations, and experiments.

Who's better at making predictions? That question isn't as easy to answer as you might think. In the past, both prophets and scientists have been right about some things—and they've also been wrong many times. Here's a look at what both kinds of future tellers have to say about the year 2000…

The future is cloudy.

I think that's a chocolate smudge.

MEET THE DOOMSDAY PROPHETS

The trouble with most prophets is that their predictions aren't exactly cheerful. Many predictions about the year 2000 have to do with floods, wars, and earthquakes—pretty scary stuff. Prophets who foresee a lot of bad news are called "doomsday" prophets.

The most famous doomsday prophet is Nostradamus, who lived in France in the 1500s. He told his predictions in riddles for people to interpret. One of his famous prophecies goes like this:

The year 1999,
month seven,
From the sky
shall come a great
king of terror…

NOSTRADAMUS

Is Nostradamus talking about the end of the world or a float in a Fourth of July parade? What do you think?

Here's what other prophets have predicted about the new millennium:

⚡ Earthquakes will cause many large areas of land to slide into the sea, including Japan, California, New York, and parts of England and Scotland.

⚡ Volcanoes all over the Pacific Ocean will erupt, burying islands in lava and ash.

⚡ A great war will wipe out the human race.

THE BRIGHT SIDE

As the year 2001 gets closer, you'll probably hear more and more prophets predicting doom. But guess what? That's exactly what happened the last time there was a new millennium. In December of 999, people predicted the end of the world would arrive at the new year. People set free their farm animals, and stores gave away their goods. On January 1, 1000, the world was still standing, and everyone felt pretty silly.

THE AMAZING CRISWELL

The sixteenth century had Nostradamus, and the twentieth century had the Amazing Criswell. Charles Criswell was a newscaster in New York. One night in the 1950s, the evening news program ran short. The producer asked Criswell to fill up the time. So Criswell predicted what the news would be the next day.

To everyone's surprise, Criswell was right! He quit the news business and became a professional prophet. None of his other predictions ever came true, but no one seemed to mind.

Criswell's most famous prediction was that aliens would take over Earth in 1999. We'll just have to wait and see…

MAKE A FINGERTIP FORTUNE-TELLER

Become a millennium predictor with your very own fortune-telling device.

HOW TO MAKE IT:

1. Cut a piece of paper into a square that's 8 1/2 inches on each side.

2. Fold in the four corners of the square so they touch in the middle. You should have a new, smaller square.

1

3. Flip over the square. Fold in the four corners again. The square should be even smaller.

2

4. Now it's time to decorate your square. Flip over the square again. Write the numbers 1, 2, 3, and 4 in the middle of the boxes.

3

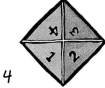

5. Now flip the square back over. Color each of the eight triangles a different color.

4

6. Now flip open each of the four large, triangle-shaped folds. Write a prediction on each side of the triangles—two for each fold. Use our predictions (on the next page) or write your own.

5

7. Now fold your fingertip fortune-teller in half. You're ready to start telling fortunes.

6

HOW TO DO IT:

1. Slip your thumbs and index fingers underneath the four flaps of paper, nestling them in the four corners. Bring your fingers together. Practice moving your fingers in and out to open the device in the center both ways.

2. Begin with your four fingers together and the fortune-teller closed. Then pick one of the numbers and open and close the fortune-teller that number of times.

3. Pick another number. Open and close the fortune-teller that number of times.

4. Now pick one of the colors showing in the fortune-teller's open position. Lift up the triangle flap. Read the prediction underneath. You've just told the future!

Use the fingertip fortune-teller with your friends and see what you predict for their futures.

PREDICTIONS TO WRITE IN FINGERTIP FORTUNE-TELLER:

- You will still be wearing the same pair of underwear in the year 2000.
- Aliens will take over the planet.
- Ice cream will be the new health food.
- A talking dog will become president of the United States.
- Giant bug people will be discovered in the center of the Earth.
- Homework will be against the law.
- Green will be the most popular hair color.
- You will become the first person to walk on Mars.

IT'S SCIENTIFIC ☑

Your fingertip fortune-teller is hardly a scientific approach to making predictions. So what ideas have scientists who actually observe, collect, and test data come up with? Keep reading to learn about some of the big things they're predicting for the new millennium.

Scientists don't rely on dreams or crystal balls. Instead, they use something called the **scientific method** to answer a question or figure out a problem. Here's how it works:

1. **OBSERVE:** The first step. What is it that you want to know more about? What problem do you want to figure out?

2. **THINK:** How many reasons can you think of that could be causing the problem? Make a guess (scientists call this a *hypothesis*).

3. **EXPERIMENT:** Find ways to test your hypothesis.

4. **MAKE CHANGES:** Chances are, your experiment won't always prove (or disprove) your hypothesis. It's okay to change your hypothesis and start again.

THE FUTURE OF ROBOTS

You've probably seen robots in movies or on television. These robots usually look like giant silver garbage cans or human-like people (think of Commander Data on *Star Trek: The Next Generation*).

Real-life robots don't have much in common with these screen creatures. But scientists are developing some pretty exciting robots for the future. Here's a preview of some of the robot news you'll be hearing about when the new millennium dawns:

ROBOTS AT WORK:

Robots that perform jobs that are dangerous or even impossible for humans to do already exist. In nuclear power plants, some robots handle hazardous waste so human workers don't have to come into contact with it. And an eight-legged robot named Dante explores the insides of volcanoes, surviving temperatures no human could withstand.

Other robots are being developed to do everyday jobs as well. Robotic arms put together products on assembly lines and even sew clothes. These robots make it possible for companies to do tasks more cheaply and efficiently, but some experts worry that an increase in these machines will put thousands of people out of work.

Has anyone invented a robot that does homework?

ROBOTS IN SPACE:
No human has ever set foot on Mars, but a robot has—in fact, two have. The *Viking Landers I* and *II* explored Mars in 1976. They wheeled across the planet and searched for signs of life with their robotic arms.

NASA (the National Aeronautic and Space Administration) has more plans for space robots in the future. Scientists at the Johnson Space Center in Houston are engineering a robot whose movements would be controlled by a human operator wearing virtual-reality gear. These robots could be used for repairing spaceships and exploring planets. Because they would be operated by a human, these robots could perform more precisely than ever before.

ANDROIDS IN THE WORKS:
Some scientists are actually working to create the human-like robots, or androids, that you see in science-fiction films. At the robot laboratory at the Massachusetts Institute of Technology, a scientist named Rodney Brooks is working on the most human-like robot to date. Its name is Cog. Why is Cog different from other robots? Brooks hopes Cog will one day see, hear, and move in the same way humans do. You probably won't see sophisticated androids until well into the next century, but Brooks thinks Cog might be the first step.

DESIGN A ROBOT

If you were a scientist, what kind of robot would you design? A useful robot to perform jobs too dangerous for humans? A fun-loving robot to hang out with? It's up to you. Use the blueprint on this page to create your very own robot. Think about what you'll need in the year 2000. Someone to drive you to school? A portable refrigerator? A walking encyclopedia to help you do homework? Draw and label the special features it will have.

ROBOT PLANS

ACME ROBOT COMPANY

DESIGNER:

NEXT STOP: SPACE!

Many scientists think the new millennium will see humans traveling farther into space than ever before. Here's what the experts are saying:

- **LUNAR VACATIONS:**

Do family trips to Grandma's bore you to tears? The future may hold something far more exciting. Experts predict that domed areas on the moon will be popular tourist attractions—maybe even during your lifetime. The only downside? It might be hard to send postcards home!

- **THE RED PLANET:**

First the moon, then Mars! Earth's neighbor is 35 million miles away. As you're reading this, researchers all over the world are exploring ways to send scientists to study the planet. Experts have created a plan to change the atmosphere on Mars so that humans could live there one day. Scientists might live in space stations there by the year 2015. After about 2150, the planet might be able to support human life on its own. Your great-great-great-great-grandchild could be a Martian!

Maybe I'll be the first Martian millipede!

- **FARTHER THAN EVER:**

Future space travelers may visit planets even farther away from Earth than Mars. With today's technology, it would take 50 years to reach the planet Pluto, a trip too long for humans to make. Experts are creating new technology that could get a spaceship there in only five years.

SAVE THE PLANET!

While scientists do predict fun things such as robots and spaceships for the future, sometimes their predictions make them sound a lot like the doomsday prophets. That usually happens when they talk about the health of planet Earth.

What's the problem? Much of it has to do with people. At the beginning of this century (1900), there were 1.7 billion people in the world. Now there are 5.7 billion! That's a big increase in a short time. And the United Nations says that by the year 2050 there might be 10 billion people on the planet.

Doubling the population would mean doubling the amount of food, water, and land that humans need. Some experts are worried that Earth won't have enough resources for all these new people.

When the first European settlers came to North America, passenger pigeons filled the skies. The settlers hunted the birds until none were left.

Even today, we 5.7 billion humans are causing problems. Chemicals we use are destroying the ozone layer, which protects Earth from the sun's harmful rays. People are pushing some animal and plant species completely out of existence.

But don't despair. The good news is that scientists are working hard to solve these problems. And of course, there's you. You don't have to be a scientist to make the future a better place to live!

MAKE A POSTER

Help spread the word about the future of planet Earth. Make a poster that shows a way that people can help manage Earth's resources. Use one of these ideas, or pick one of your own.

- **CONSERVATION:** Your poster could show ways to save energy and water.

- **THE THREE Rs: REDUCE, REUSE, RECYCLE!** Being smart about what we make and buy can help save resources.

- **ENDANGERED ANIMALS:** Find out more about animals that are in danger of becoming extinct and what can be done to save them.

- **GO GREEN:** Use your poster to start a campaign to plant gardens and trees in your community.

SCIENCE FICTION

Somewhere between the mystical world of prophets and the serious world of scientists lies the world of science fiction. For about 200 years, writers have been combining scientific facts with their imaginations to create visions of the future. Sometimes they've been right on target.

Meet two men whose sci-fi visions have amazed the world:

JULES VERNE

Born in 1828 in France, Jules Verne was always dreaming of strange, faraway places. When he was eleven, Verne tried to stow away on a ship so he could travel the world.

Jules Verne wrote over 50 novels!

Later in life, Verne became a writer and used his imagination to take him to fantastic places. In 1865, he wrote *Journey from the Earth to the Moon*. Verne wasn't the first to write about space travel, but his book predicted some amazing things. The rocket in his

SCI-FI ON THE SCREEN

These days, science fiction is as popular as ever, especially on television and in the movies. Some science-fiction shows focus on the far-off future. But some have explored the new millennium.

The movie *2001: A Space Odyssey* was about astronauts who encounter alien life in space. There are no scaly aliens with antennae in this movie, though. The alien life form is shown as a giant black pillar. Released in 1968, the movie contained a warning about the new millennium. In the film, a power-hungry computer goes out of control, showing viewers what could happen if technology is not kept in check.

Space: 1999 was a popular television show in the late 1970s. It featured a group of space explorers traveling the galaxy. The catchy title of the show is evidence that people were starting to get excited about the new millennium over twenty years ago!

23

book was launched from Florida—exactly where space missiles are launched from today! Verne also predicted that animals would be sent into space on test flights.

In *20,000 Leagues Under the Sea,* written in 1870, Verne came up with the idea of an amazing ship that could travel underwater. Twenty-eight years later, an American man named Simon Lake was inspired by Verne's concept, and he invented the first submarine.

H. G. WELLS

Herbert George Wells lived in England and wrote books around the same time as Jules Verne. Like Verne, Wells wrote about moon exploration in his book, *First Men in the Moon,* published in 1901.

But Wells also wrote about some incredible things that haven't happened—yet. He was the first person to think about the possibility of creating a machine that could travel through time. And his book *War of the Worlds* is the story of a Martian invasion of Earth. Though scientists have proven that there is no life on Mars, Wells's story of aliens was convincing. In 1938, people listening to a radio play based on the book thought that we really were being attacked by Martians, and there was temporary panic in parts of the country. Today, many people still wonder if there is life in other places in the universe.

24

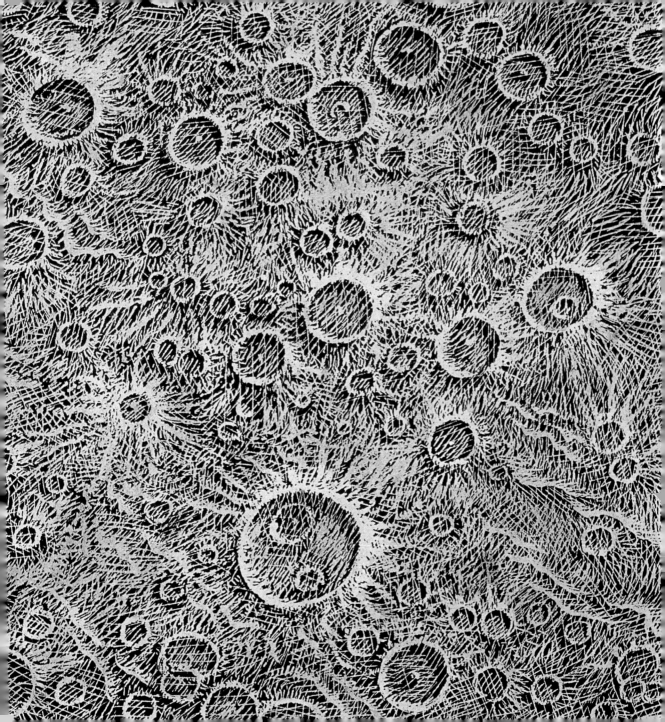

WRITE A SCI-FI STORY

Follow in the steps of Jules Verne and H. G. Wells. Cut out each box in this grid of sci-fi words and put them into a bag or a hat. Pick five words. Now use them all to write a science-fiction story.

worm people	time machine	warp speed
black hole	space buggy	king lizard
jet pack	alien	hover car
robot	comet dust	rocket ship
Mars	antigravity suit	astronaut
red zone	scientist	space colony
cosmic slime	meteor monster	moon

MAKE PREDICTIONS 👁

You've heard what scientists, prophets, and writers have had to say about the new millennium. Now it's your turn. What do you think the future holds? Write your predictions on this page. Read your predictions on each New Year's Day between now and the year 2001. Have any of your predictions come true? Have you changed your mind? Update your predictions as you go.

MY PREDICTIONS ABOUT SPACE
TRAVEL: _____

_____

Updates: 1997: _____

1998: _____

1999: _____

2000: _____

2001: Will send people to
Mars

MY PREDICTIONS ABOUT THE
ENVIRONMENT: _____

_____

Updates: 1997: _____

1998: _____

1999: _____

2000: _____

2001: _____

MY PREDICTIONS ABOUT WORLD
POPULATION: _____

_____

Updates: 1997: _____

1998: _____

1999: _____

2000: _____

2001: The violence will not
be as much because
the population will
be lower.

ONE THOUSAND YEARS AGO

It's fun to think about the fantastic possibilities of the future. But to see where we're going, it helps to see where we've been. So first we'll take a quick trip to the past, to the year 1000, to see how far we've come since the last millennium.

One thousand years is a long time. What was life like for a typical kid in the year 1000?

CENTRAL EUROPE, 1000

About 90 percent of people in Europe during this time lived on farms called manors. If you were lucky, your father was a lord who owned the manor house. But chances are you belonged to one of the many peasant families who tended the crops on the lord's land in exchange for protection from raiders and barbarians.

Spring: As soon as the cold ground thaws, it's time to hit the fields. It doesn't matter if you're a man or a woman, young or old; your days are spent planting grains and other vegetables on the lord's land. When your planting's done, you'll try to find time to tend to the small garden next to the thatched hut your family lives in. You may also have to help your mother milk the lord's cows and gather the eggs from the lord's chickens.

Summer: There's no time to rest in summer. Now that the crops are growing, the fields need to be weeded and cared for. In August, it's time to start harvesting the hay that will be fed to the lord's livestock. It's hard work, and the sun is hot, but you can't stop until all the hay is harvested. This usually takes until the middle of September!

Fall: Now that the food is harvested, it's time to prepare it for winter. You must grind wheat into flour; you crush grapes and make them into wine. If you're lucky, the lord will give you a portion of the harvest big enough to last you through the winter. If not, you'll have to hope that the harvest from your own small garden does the job. And don't even think about going to school—there's no such thing as public education. Just about the only people who are taught to read and write are men of the church.

28

Winter: Men may get a short break when cold weather sets in, but not women! Mothers and daughters spend the short days cooking for their families and for the lord, weaving cloth, and making clothes. In February, when the days get a little longer, the men begin sharpening their tools in preparation for a new planting season.

Life was different for people in different parts of the world in the year 1000:

GHANA, AFRICA
This was an exciting time to be in this African country. The capital city of Kumbi was the heart of a huge trading empire. Jewelry, weapons, cloth, ivory, pearls, cattle, and horses were all sold in the crowded market-places there.

NORTH AMERICA
In the year 1000, the Anasazi Indian tribe was thriving in what is now New Mexico. These people built elaborate, multistory dwellings into the sides of desert canyons. They grew corn, squash, and beans.

MAKE A DIARY FOR THE FUTURE

Try to imagine yourself a few years from now. Write what you'll do, eat, wear, and think on a typical day in the year 2000. (You might want to do this for one school day and one summer day.) When the year 2000 does come, look back at what you wrote. How far off was your prediction?

6 A.M. _____

_____

8 A.M. _____

_____

10 A.M. _____

_____

noon _____

_____

2 P.M. _____

_____

4 P.M. _____

_____

6 P.M. _____

_____

8 P.M. _____

_____

10 P.M. _____

_____

midnight _____

_____

FAR INTO THE FUTURE

Imagining yourself in the year 2000 wasn't that hard, was it? But what happens when you travel even farther into the future? What do you think a typical day might be like for a kid in the year **3000**? How different do you think it might be from your life now?

6 A.M. _____

8 A.M. _____

10 A.M. _____

noon _____

2 P.M. _____

4 P.M. _____

6 P.M. _____

8 P.M. _____

10 P.M. _____

midnight _____

WHAT WILL _YOUR_ LIFE BE LIKE?

GETTING DOWN TO BASICS

Now it's time to find out how _your_ life will be affected by the coming of the new millennium.

What will the school cafeteria be serving in the next thousand years (or even the next hundred)?

What will you be rushing to the store to buy just to keep up with the latest fashions? Will there still be stores to rush to?

Will you still be living in your house or apartment, or will you be shuttled into space to live in a space station? Read on to find out the answers to these (and other) questions.

Although most of us want to surround ourselves with all kinds of creature comforts, there are really only three basic things we need to survive: food, clothing, and shelter. Sure, you might think you could _never_ live without your stereo, compact disc player, or television set, but face it—you really could. In fact, people who lived at the beginning of this century never even heard of those things.

WHAT'S FOR DINNER?

Let's start at the beginning of our "basics" list: food. Imagine that it's about six-thirty, and you're called in for dinner. Your stomach is growling, and you can't wait to sink your teeth into that juicy burger you just know will be sitting on your plate. You rush into the dining room and do a double take. What is that thing—that *speck*—sitting on your plate? It's your dinner, of course—in the form of a handy pill. No need for napkins. No need to dirty dishes. You just need a glass of water to wash it down, and voilà! You have all the vitamins, minerals, and calories you need.

Sound crazy?

Maybe. But not so long ago, some people thought that by the year 2000 our meals would be reduced to a pill or two. Now that idea seems kind of silly. Still, even though we're not eating meals-in-a-pill yet, our eating habits have changed over the years and will continue to change as time goes on.

Will there be enough food to go around in the new millennium? (On page 21 we talked about how the world's population is growing. All those new people will need to eat!) Some experts say the earth has more than enough resources to feed 11 billion people—and more. Still, according to some estimates, 700 million people suffer from malnutrition. This is not because the world does not *produce* enough food, but because poor nations do not have enough money to buy it. So nations around the world are working to make sure that food is produced without hurting the environment and that the food reaches the people who really need it (see page 36). What about your community? Is everyone who needs food getting it?

FOOD AND YOU

So, what will you be eating in the new millennium? Grab your knife and fork and check out some trends:

• LOTS OF GREENS Thinking about becoming a vegetarian? If you make that choice, you won't be alone. According to some surveys, more than 40 percent of teenage girls and over 15 percent of teenage boys (and almost 50 percent of female college students) think not eating meat is "in." And it is thought that these numbers will grow as we approach the year 2000.

• NEW FOOD COMBINATIONS As ethnic populations grow in the United States, expect to see some new and *unique* food combinations, including moo shu pork burritos, pitas stuffed with pizza toppings, and potato skins served with salsa.

• SNACKS Munchies will still be popular in the years to come. According to one survey, pretzels are fast becoming the nation's favorite snack food, with tortilla chips a close second.

• MEALS AT THE MOVIES Forget the popcorn and the jujubes. In the new millennium, you'll be able to munch on pizza and tacos while enjoying your favorite flick.

• NO MORE MYSTERY MEAT The lunch bell rings. You race to your school cafeteria and grab a tray. But you're in for a big surprise! Instead of getting mystery meat on a bun plopped on your plate, you're given a double burger with cheese, french fries, and a shake! Yes, in the new millennium, many schools will serve your favorite fast food (direct from your favorite fast-food restaurants) for lunch. In fact, your school may be doing this already.

CREATE A MENU FOR THE NEW MILLENNIUM

It's the year 2001. Your best friend is coming over for dinner, and there's *nothing* in the house to eat. Your robot-chef has volunteered to do the cooking, but it's up to you to plan the menu:

FUTURE FOOD

Scientists are always coming up with new and better ways of producing food. Take genetic engineering, for example. Genetic engineering is a process that alters the genes (the hereditary material) in an organism. By changing that chemical information, scientists can create new and better varieties of plants. They hope that this will increase the quality and quantity of the world's food supply. So in the new millennium, you can expect to see a lot of genetically engineered food on the supermarket shelves. These are some of the things that scientists have been doing already:

• A synthetic growth hormone known as *recombinant bovine somatotropin* (you can call it rBST) was one of the first products of genetic engineering to be approved for use in food production. A growth hormone is a substance that controls the process by which something matures. Cows who were given rBST increased their milk production by about 15 percent. That means more people can be fed by the same cow.

• Certain types of corn have been genetically engineered so that they can protect themselves against plant pests. The corn that you see growing in large fields is sometimes eaten, or even totally destroyed, by certain insects. The new hybrid corn has been altered to produce a protein that guards against these nasty pests.

• In 1994, the "Flavr Savr" tomato hit the market. The Flavr Savr tomato has an "antisense" gene that slows the biological process by which it ripens, softens, and eventually rots. So this genetically engineered tomato can stay on the vine longer before being harvested and can still remain firm enough to ship. Most other tomatoes are picked and shipped while green and hard.

Then they are exposed to ethylene gas, which causes them to turn pink. The Flavr Savr tomatoes don't have to be exposed to any kind of gas.

Supporters of genetic engineering say that these new methods will provide healthier, cheaper, and better-tasting food. Also, farmers won't have to use toxic chemicals to control weeds and pests, because the genetically engineered food will already be immune to those. But best of all, supporters say that genetic engineering will increase the world's food supply to meet the needs of our growing population.

Some researchers are looking into creating bananas and potatoes that contain built-in vaccines for diseases.

Sounds good, you say? Well, wait until you hear the other side before you decide. Critics say that as a result of genetic engineering, allergy-producing proteins may spread more widely through the food supply. They're also afraid that this technology has the power to create ecological disasters, such as fast-growing weeds, oversized fish that eat everything in sight, and plant viruses.

So what happens if you get sick from eating this "future food"? In the new millennium, there may be no need for x-rays or exploratory surgery. Scientists are working on developing a "super-stethoscope" that will use ultrasound to let doctors "see" inside your body.

And if you do end up on the operating table, the human hands of a doctor might not be the only ones working on you. Some experts believe that certain operations may be performed by robots controlled by human surgeons.

WHAT WILL YOU WEAR?

People started wearing clothing more than 100,000 years ago. Why? Probably for the same reasons you wear clothing: to protect yourself from the cold and the heat, to make yourself look good, and to tell others something about yourself.

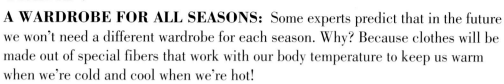

MILLENNIUM FASHION TRENDS

A WARDROBE FOR ALL SEASONS: Some experts predict that in the future we won't need a different wardrobe for each season. Why? Because clothes will be made out of special fibers that work with our body temperature to keep us warm when we're cold and cool when we're hot!

SPACE SUITS: Other fashion experts predict that in the new millennium we will see "space-age fashion." Sterile white clothing decorated with shiny metal will be hanging in every store window.

TO DO

Of course, people have worn many different types of clothing throughout the ages. In fact, *you've* probably worn lots of different types of clothing throughout *your* lifetime. Styles of clothing come and go. One year, short skirts and belly-baring tops might be in, and the next year, they might be totally out. Can you think of some things you wore years ago that you wouldn't be caught dead in today? Make a list (and include some drawings) of some of the weird and not-so-weird clothing you've worn:

MY FIRST PAIR OF SHOES: (You may have to ask an adult or look at some old photos to describe these.)

WHAT I WORE MY FIRST DAY OF SCHOOL: (We're talking about preschool or kindergarten here. Again, you may have to ask for help.)

SOMETHING(S) I WAS FORCED TO WEAR (THAT I'D LIKE TO FORGET ABOUT):

So what kind of clothing can you expect in the new millennium? Television shows and movies that depict the future often show people wearing functional jumpsuits or metallic space wear. Right now, however, people tend to wear variations of older clothing styles. So perhaps in the future we'll go back to the past for our fashions. Maybe you'll be wearing some of these clothes in the new millennium:

- **SKIRTS FOR MEN** The clothing of choice for many Egyptian men was skirts. Most of the time, they wore one skirt on top of another. But the skirts-for-men fashion craze didn't end with the Egyptians. The Cretans, who lived on Crete (an island about 80 miles south of Greece) wore skirts, too. Their skirts were short and were held up at the waist by tight belts.

- **TOGAS!** In ancient Greece and Rome, men and women wore *togas,* large pieces of cloth worn over one or both shoulders.

- **WHAT'S A WIMPLE?** During the 1100s and 1200s, European women wore *metal* hair nets, veils, and draped throat coverings called *wimples.* That must have been hot!

- **BULGING BELLIES** During the 1500s, European men wore something called a *peasecod belly,* which had a pointed bulge over the stomach. Lots of room for those extra-big meals!

- **MEN'S WEAR** By about 1660, some men in Europe started wearing huge, curly wigs called *periwigs.* They also wore high-heeled shoes and silk stockings trimmed with bows and lace.

- **TIGHT-FITTING CLOTHES** Many women in nineteenth-century America would have worn tight *corsets*—underwear belts that pulled in their waists very tightly—and great big round skirts that were held out by a hoop.

I can't breathe!

- **ZOOT SUITS** During the 1930s and 1940s, it was fashionable for American men to wear *zoot suits.* A zoot suit consisted of a baggy jacket that reached to the knees and baggy pants that came up as far as the chest. With it, stylish men sometimes wore a long chain that hung down from the chest, suspenders, and a floppy hat.

- **PAINTED STOCKINGS** During World War II, there wasn't enough silk to make stockings. (Before there were panty hose or nylons, women wore silk stockings that had a seam up the back.) So to make it look as though they were wearing stockings, women painted lines on the backs of their legs to look like seams.

CLOTHES DRYER OF THE FUTURE

Experts say that soon we'll have a clothes dryer that will save 20 percent of the energy used by regular dryers and will cut the drying time by two-thirds. What kind of machine could do that? A *microwave* clothes dryer! This new microwave dryer will only get as hot as 110 degrees Fahrenheit and will steam your clothes. A regular dryer, on the other hand, can reach 350 degrees Fahrenheit—essentially baking your clothes.

- **MINISKIRTS** These very, very short skirts became popular for women in the 1960s. Since then, hemlines have gone back down and back up several times.

- **BELL BOTTOMS AND PLATFORMS**
During the 1970s, both men and women wore pants with really wide bottoms, called *bell bottoms,* and big platform shoes. Some platform shoes even had live goldfish swimming in the hollow, water-filled platforms.

CHART THE TRENDS

Use the chart that follows to keep track of your own fashion trends—the kinds of clothes you're wearing, what your hair looks like, and what's hot and what's not—as we approach the beginning of the new millennium. You can also use the chart to *predict* future styles. Make predictions for the years that follow the current one. Then, when that year arrives, check your predictions. Were you right? You may give yourself a big laugh!

MY FAVORITE CLOTHES RIGHT NOW: _____

_____

MY FAVORITE PAIR OF SHOES RIGHT NOW: _____

_____

WHAT'S IN: _____

_____

WHAT'S OUT: _____

_____

1997:

WHAT I PREDICT:

What kinds of clothes will I wear? _____
_____

What kinds of shoes will I wear? _____
_____

What will be in: _____
_____

What will be out: _____
_____

WHAT REALLY HAPPENED:

Kinds of clothes I wear: _____
_____

Kinds of shoes I wear: _____
_____

What is in: _____
_____

What is out: _____
_____

1998:

WHAT I PREDICT:

What kinds of clothes will I wear?
_____

What kinds of shoes will I wear? _____
_____

What will be in: _____
_____

What will be out: _____

WHAT REALLY HAPPENED:

Kinds of clothes I wear:
_____

Kinds of shoes I wear: _____
_____

What is in: _____
_____

What is out: _____

1999:

WHAT I PREDICT:

What kinds of clothes will I wear?
_____

What kinds of shoes will I wear? _____
_____

WHAT REALLY HAPPENED:

Kinds of clothes I wear:
_____

Kinds of shoes I wear: _____
_____

1999 CONTINUED:

WHAT I PREDICT:

What will be in: _____

_____

What will be out: _____

_____

WHAT REALLY HAPPENED:

What is in: _____

_____

What is out: _____

_____

2000:

WHAT I PREDICT:

What kinds of clothes will I wear? _____

_____

What kinds of shoes will I wear? _____

_____

What will be in: _____

_____

What will be out: _____

_____

WHAT REALLY HAPPENED:

Kinds of clothes I wear: _____

_____

Kinds of shoes I wear: _____

_____

What is in: _____

_____

What is out: _____

_____

2001:

WHAT I PREDICT:

What kinds of clothes will I wear? _____

_____

What kinds of shoes will I wear? _____

_____

What will be in: _____

_____

What will be out: _____

_____

WHAT REALLY HAPPENED:

Kinds of clothes I wear: _____

_____

Kinds of shoes I wear: _____

_____

What is in: _____

_____

What is out: _____

_____

45

SHOPPING

So now you know what you might be eating and wearing in the new millennium. But where will you get your food and clothing? Gone are the days when people grow *all* their own food and make *all* their own clothing. Today, people get their goods from a variety of sources: the corner store, the strip mall, the mega-mall, mail-order catalogs, and home-shopping television shows.

The way we shop is constantly changing. Picture this: you're sitting at home when your mom reminds you it's your turn to do the weekly family grocery shopping. No problem. You pull out your remote control and call up your grocery list on your television screen. You add a few more items—a gallon of milk, a bunch of broccoli, a gallon of ice cream. Then you press the "send" button. Your order will be delivered to your house in 50 minutes.

Sound far-fetched? Some experts predict that by the year 2004,

interactive home shopping will rake in a whopping $300 billion a year. And this kind of shopping won't be limited to grocery items. You'll be able to get anything—from a new pair of sneakers to a new stereo system—with a flick of your remote.

So, will "regular" shopping stores disappear in the next millennium? Probably not. But the big stores that do stick around will not only be there to service you but to entertain you as well. Superstores and mega-malls will come fully equipped with restaurants, multiplex movie theaters, miniature theme parks, waterfalls, and more!

Superstores are extra-large versions of places such as bookstores or hardware stores. They house tons of merchandise and often have space for sitting, places to interact with the merchandise, and huge displays.

SHOP WITH YOUR COMPUTER, TOO!

Thanks to the internet and the world-wide web, some experts predict you'll never have to visit the mall again. Through your computer, you'll be able to visit any store in the world. You'll actually get to "walk" through the store's doors and down the aisles, picking out all the clothes (or other merchandise) you want. Then the clothes will be delivered to your house (for a price, of course!)

In case you don't already know, here's the scoop on the internet. Listen up, because it's going to be a *big* part of your life in the new millennium:

The internet was created by the Defense Department in the 1950s. More recently, the Defense Department realized it didn't have much use for it, so it offered the internet to college professors. The college professors showed the internet to students, and voilà—it took off! (Of course, we're simplifying things a bit here.)

On the internet are things called websites, where you can get lots of information. You can use the internet to explore interactive encyclopedias, talk to kids in other countries, even talk to scientists at NASA. So get prepared—the internet is coming to you.

THE FUTURE IS NOW
The Mall of America, located in Minneapolis, Minnesota, has become one of that city's major tourist attractions. Opened in 1992 on a 78-acre site, the mall includes 4 department stores, over 400 specialty stores, a 7-acre amusement park (including a roller coaster), a 14-screen movie complex, 45 restaurants, 9 nightclubs, a wedding chapel, a play center, and an 18-hole miniature golf course!

POLL TIME!

Take a poll of your friends and relatives, asking them which they would prefer: video shopping or mall shopping. The results may help you predict which will be more popular in the future.

VIDEO SHOPPING | MALL SHOPPING

total # of video shopping

total # of mall shopping

GO GET A JOB

Face it—if you want to shop, you've got to have money. And in order to get money, you've got to get a job. So what kinds of jobs will be available in the year 2000 and beyond? Start thinking about these fields:

• **BIOTECHNOLOGY** This is the study of the relationship between humans and machines. As machines become a bigger part of our lives, we'll need people to study how we interact together.

• **COMPUTER PROGRAMMING** This will be a hot field—but only until the year 2005 or so. According to some sources, after that computer programming will become automated, and there will be no need to hire people to program.

• **ENVIRONMENTAL CLEANUP** According to some experts, in the next millennium, 40 percent of the world's water will be polluted. So lots of people will be needed to help clean it up!

• **NANOTECHNOLOGY** Nano *what?* Nanotechnology is the technique of building microscopic machines one molecule at a time. If you like detail, this is the field for you!

• **HEALTH CARE** The baby boomers (people born after World War II and before 1964) will start retiring in the year 2010. This group will probably need medical attention, so there will be a great demand for more home-care aides and other health workers.

SHELTER

Pop quiz: what else do you need to survive besides food and clothing? Shelter! A shelter is a structure that provides protection against bad weather or danger. There are many people in this world who don't have shelter, but that doesn't mean they don't need it.

The first shelters made by people were built from animal hides, stones, straw, vines, or wood. Today, people make shelter from lots of different materials: wood, brick, steel, concrete, aluminum, glass, and plastic. What is your house or apartment building made of? How about the other shelters in your neighborhood?

QUESTION-AND-ANSWER TIME

Ask your parents, grandparents, or some other older relative or friend what their houses looked like when they were growing up. Write a description below: _____

_____

_____

How does the house (or houses) you described above compare to the place you live now? Below, write a description of your home. You can paste a photo (or draw a picture) next to your description. _____

_____

_____

_____

_____

_____

_____

MORE SHELTER INFO

What will shelter be like in the new millennium? Here are some of the things that are on the drafting table:

- **LOTS OF GREEN IN BETWEEN** Some people think that since we have used so many of our natural resources (such as trees for lumber for new structures), we're going to spend the new millennium protecting what's left of our natural environment. When we rebuild our neighborhoods (or build new ones), we'll pay special attention to the green space between buildings. Architects will make it a priority to plan for trees or bushes to be planted in business and housing developments.

- **RECYCLED BUILDINGS** Recycled materials (such as glass and plastic) will be used more often when we build new buildings.

- **MULTIFUNCTION BUILDINGS** Some experts predict that one building will take on several functions in the future. Instead of standing empty after five o'clock, an office building might be used as an adult education center in the evening and an exercise studio in the early morning. School buildings, especially, will probably be used more like community centers. Neighborhoods will use a nearby school for meetings, performances, and community events.

Other researchers believe that in the twenty-first century, people will be relocating more than they do now. So buildings might be used more like hotels, where anyone can live and work in comfort.

- **HOUSE OF THE FUTURE** Arthur C. Clarke, one of the world's best-known science-fiction authors, envisions that the home of the new millennium will take care of its owner's every need. Your house would sense your mood, adjust the blinds, select your music, and even brew your coffee with just the amount of caffeine you like.

GOTTA GET THERE!

No matter where you live, you'll have to leave your house sometime. So how will you get to the places you want to go in the next millennium? Here are some ideas for the future:

• **EFFICIENT CARS** Car makers plan to develop a car that is three times more fuel efficient than today's car. It will also be virtually emissions free (no more ugly discharges!).

• **SMART CARS** Cars will have built-in navigation systems that will tell drivers the best route and warn them about delays or accidents. Cars will also come equipped with special sensors in the bumpers and frame that will help drivers sense (and avoid) accidents. And if an accident does occur, the car will automatically call for help.

• **BETTER PUBLIC TRANSPOR-TATION** At train or bus stations, you will be able to buy tickets and get directions at interactive kiosks (booths). Buses will be made out of lightweight, high-strength material and will be powered by natural gas, hydrogen, or

In 1957, a plastic "House of the Future" was built at Disneyland. At that time, most people thought that plastic was the material of the future. In 1967, the house was sup-posed to be torn down—but the wrecking ball bounced right off the surface! Workers ended up demolishing it by hand.

even electric batteries! And like the smart cars, buses will also be equipped with de-vices to sense and avoid potential crashes.

• **CONTROLLED HIGHWAYS** You won't have to worry about having to keep to the speed limit when you drive, because the highway will do it for you! Special sensors and communication devices will actually guide cars along the road.

DESIGN A HOUSE OF THE FUTURE

What do you think houses of the future will look like? Will they have many rooms or just one big room? Will houses be filled with computers and robots to help meet your every need? Now it's your turn to make a prediction! How will people in the next millennium shelter themselves?

Take out your pencils and design a house of the future.

HOUSE of the FUTURE

THERE'S ALWAYS TIME FOR FUN!

There may be only three things you need to survive—food, clothing, and shelter—but it's nice to have entertainment, too! And the form of entertainment that will change most radically in the new millennium is television. So hold onto your remote and check out what changes are in store for the next ten or twenty years:

• **MORE CHANNELS**—Thanks to fiber-optic wires, up to a thousand channels will be delivered to your televisions.

• **NEW STRATEGIES**—Networks will start using something called "multiplexing," with one network offering several options at the same time. For example, on Wednesday night at eight o'clock, ABC-One might show a movie, while ABC-Two shows a sporting event, and ABC-Three shows a sitcom.

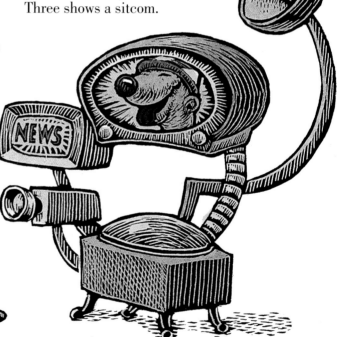

- **INTERACTIVE TV**—You'll be able to do lots of cool things with interactive television, including picking the ending of your favorite television show or film, choosing camera angles and shots you'd like to see, and getting information on demand, such as the song lyrics to the music video you're watching.

- **VIRTUAL REALITY**—With virtual-reality equipment that can be hooked up to your television, you'll be able to feel like you're actually participating in a television program by being able to interact in a computer-driven environment. You could go out for a pass from your favorite quarterback!

- **HIGH-DEFINITION TELEVISION**—You think you get a good picture now on your television? You haven't seen anything yet! Look out for wide-screen formats with amazingly sharp clarity and sound.

- **NO MORE CARTRIDGES**—You'll be able to play an unlimited number of video games right on your television. Special channels will be devoted only to video games.

- **VIDEO ON DEMAND**—With the flick of a button, you'll be able to see any video-movie that you want (for a price, of course!).

- **SET-TOP BOX**—This device will function as a cable converter and a personal computer—all in one! You'll be able to look through entertainment libraries with hundreds of titles, browse through home-shopping catalogs, play video games, and send and receive messages to other people who have set-top boxes.

TRACK YOUR TELEVISION VIEWING HABITS

On the chart below, keep track of your current television viewing habits. Make some predictions, too. What changes will happen to television, and when will they happen?

NUMBER OF CHANNELS MY TELEVISION HAS:

1996: _____

1997: Prediction: _____   Actual: _____

1998: Prediction: _____   Actual: _____

1999: Prediction: _____   Actual: _____

2000: Prediction: _____   Actual: _____

2001: Prediction: _____   Actual: _____

TOP TELEVISION SHOWS:

1996: _____

1997: Prediction: _____   Actual: _____

1998: Prediction: _____   Actual: _____

1999: Prediction: _____   Actual: _____

2000: Prediction: _____   Actual: _____

2001: Prediction: _____   Actual: _____

THINGS I CAN DO ON MY TELEVISION BESIDES WATCHING TELEVISION PROGRAMS:

1996: _____

1997: Prediction: _____   Actual: _____

1998: Prediction: _____   Actual: _____

1999: Prediction: _____   Actual: _____

2000: Prediction: _____   Actual: _____

2001: Prediction: _____   Actual: _____

NUMBER OF HOURS I SPEND WATCHING TELEVISION PER DAY:

1996: _____

1997: Prediction: _____   Actual: _____

1998: Prediction: _____   Actual: _____

1999: Prediction: _____   Actual: _____

2000: Prediction: _____   Actual: _____

2001: Prediction: _____   Actual: _____

WRITE YOUR OWN SITCOM

Write the pilot episode for a television sitcom that takes place in the future. Will your show take place in 2010? 2500? 2999? Who will your main characters be? (Will they even be human?) Where will they be living? What will they wear? What kinds of jobs and problems will they have? Be wild. Be wacky. Have fun!

CELEBRATE!

Grab some confetti. Take out your noise-makers. Put on your party hats. It's time to plan your New Year's celebration! This won't be your run-of-the-mill party, where everyone watches the ball drop in Times Square and then kisses the person standing next to them. No, sir. This will be the party to end all parties. We won't just be ringing in a new year—we'll be ringing in a new millennium!

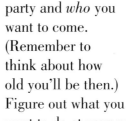

Remember, the new millennium begins in 2001, and the old one ends in 2000. Even though you might not officially ring in the new millennium until December 31, 2000, the big party is probably going to be on December 31, 1999.

It's never too soon to start planning a party, even if you have to make some changes as the big day approaches. First, decide *where* you're going to have your party and *who* you want to come. (Remember to think about how old you'll be then.) Figure out what you want to do at your party. (And even if you really don't plan on having a party, it can be fun imagining what your New Year's party *could* be like.) Use the chart on the next page to help you plan.

MAKE A 2001 PARTY PLAN

I PLAN TO INVITE THE FOLLOWING PEOPLE TO MY PARTY:
_____

_____

MY PARTY WILL BE HELD AT: _____

THINGS TO DO AT THE PARTY (GAMES, MUSIC, ETC.): _____
_____

SUPPLIES I'LL NEED: _____
_____

HERE'S MY INVITATION:

KEEP A RECORD: YOU AND YOUR WORLD

A lot of things could (and probably *will*) happen to you between now and the time the year 2001 arrives. Use these pages to keep track of the ever-changing you and your surrounding world.

ME:

Height	Weight
1996: _____	_____
1997: _____	_____
1998: _____	_____
1999: _____	_____
2000: _____	_____
2001: _____	_____

MY FRIENDS:

1996: _____

_____

1997: _____

_____

1998: _____

_____

1999: _____

_____

2000: _____

_____

2001: _____

_____

MY FAVORITE SUBJECT(S):

1996: _____

_____

1997: _____

_____

1998: _____

_____

1999: _____

_____

2000: _____

_____

2001: _____

_____

MY FAVORITE TEACHER(S):

1996: _____

_____

1997: _____

_____

1998: _____

_____

1999: _____

_____

2000: _____

_____

2001: _____

_____

TOP SONGS:

1996: _____

_____

1997: _____

_____

1998: _____

(TOP SONGS, 1998 CONTINUED)

_____

1999: _____

_____

2000: _____

_____

2001: _____

_____

TOP MOVIES:

1996: _____

_____

1997: _____

_____

1998: _____

_____

1999: _____

_____

2000: _____

_____

2001: _____

_____

POPULAR BOOKS:

1996: _____

_____

1997: _____

_____

1998: _____

_____

1999: _____

_____

2000: _____

_____

2001 _____

_____

IMPORTANT NATIONAL AND WORLD EVENTS:

1996: _____

_____

1997: _____

_____

1998: _____

_____

1999: _____

_____

2000: _____

_____

2001: _____

_____

_____

PICTURES OF ME:

LOCAL KID DOES GOOD